Search Ads

B. Vincent

Published by RWG Publishing, 2021.

While every precaution has been taken in the preparation of this book, the publisher assumes no responsibility for errors or omissions, or for damages resulting from the use of the information contained herein.

SEARCH ADS

First edition. August 10, 2021.

Copyright © 2021 B. Vincent.

Written by B. Vincent.

Also by B. Vincent

Bookkeeping
Bridge Pages
Business Acquisition
Business Bogging
Marketing Automation
Better Meetings
Business Conflict Resolution
Conversion Optimization
Creative Solutions
Employee Recruitment
Startup Capital
Employee Mentoring
Followership
Servant Leadership
Human Resources
Team Building
Freelancing
Funnel Building
Geo Targeting
Goal Setting
Immanent List Building
Lead Generation
Leadership Course
Leadership Transition
LinkedIn Ads
LinkedIn Marketing
Messenger Marketing
New Management
Newsfeed Ads
Search Ads
Online Learning

Sales Webinars
Side Hustles
Split Testing
Twitter Timeline Advertising

Table of Contents

Search Ads

Hi and welcome to this seminar on search publicizing. What's more, this course we will cover how to set up paid pursuit ads with Google promotion words. This course is isolated into three modules, module one covers advertisement crusade objectives, module two covers promotion gatherings and catchphrases and module three covers making the advertisements and observing execution. When this course is finished. You'll realize how to successfully dispatch internet searcher advertisement crusades and acquire monstrous traffic to your business. So, moving along, how about we jump into the main module. Hi, and welcome to module one. In this module, our advertisement master will show you the different mission objectives and how to pick the best ones for your business. So, prepare to take a few notes and we should directly bounce in.

Module One

O K. So, I'm going to and walk You through the different objectives you can browse while making an inquiry advertisement crusade in Google promotions. We'll begin here at the principal dashboard, and we'll click crusades up here on the left. This carries us to our mission dashboard. What's more, since We need to make the upgraded one, we'll click this blue in addition to sign catch here on the left-hand side, and we'll choose new mission.

As should be obvious, we have seven objectives to browse, yet first Let's discussion about what the word objective really implies in the advertisement Words universe you see, as opposed to allow organizations to fight for themselves and attempt to sort out every little factor and alternative in their promotion settings without completely getting what they do. Google concluded as of late to assist with directing publicists along in understanding and molding their promotions to streamline them for explicit normal showcasing objectives. So, in the event that you pick one of these objectives, you'll see accommodating little ideas close to every one of the settings and alternatives in the impending advances, ideas explicitly custom-made towards your objective. It takes a great deal of the mystery out of the promotion creation measure, which already could be Pretty confounding. Presently, remember, you need to pick the primary concern you need to achieve with this specific promotion crusade.

We should examine every one first up their business, Google advertisements Words can assist you with bringing deals through a huge number of channels, including on the web stores, deal pages, inside applications via telephone, and surprisingly genuinely coming up. Presently you'll see down here, a rundown of mission types related with each mission objective. This could be either search advertisements, show promotions, shopping advertisements, video promotions, or all-inclusive application advertisements. Since this course is about search publicizing yet need to ensure any objective, we select has search as a material mission type, which You can see deals does next there's leads This is tied in with getting possibilities onto your rundown Building a fundamental Email list or accomplishing more confounded lead age where you're gathering telephone numbers, locations, or whatever else. This objective will assist you with upgrading your advertisement for greatest return. Since this objective, principal center point is transformation following. It doesn't restrict you to conventional lead age. This can likewise assist you with advancing different activities like enrolling for an online class or taking a review.

Next, we have site traffic. Presently this objective is ostensibly the most nonexclusive and least explicit. I would Say this would best serve individuals who are doing content promoting or simply attempting to get more eyeballs on their blog entries and who don't actually think often about explicit activities or transformations, however it very well may be utilized for an entire host of things. Then, at that point there's item and brand thought. This is a profoundly particular Type of objective.

That is generally arranged towards potential clients who have effectively begun their exploration Process. What's more, you need to recognize your items or administrations from others and urge them to investigate more about your answers. There's much more potential for commitment inside the promotion. With this objective. For instance, you Can make intelligent light boxes and advertisements with different pictures that They can communicate with. It's really cool, yet as you can see, this objective is simply material to the presentation and video crusade types, not search advertisements, so we can skip it brand mindfulness and arrive at this. One's about sees. In the event that individuals click your advertisements, that's extraordinary, yet we're truly centered around individuals seeing, seeing, and becoming mindful of your image, your name, your logo, your novel selling suggestion, as you can likely estimate these are exceptionally visual promotions. Furthermore, as such hunt is indeed, not one of the relevant mission types. So, we can avoid This next application advancement. This current one's quite direct. You need individuals to introduce and utilize your applications. This one depends on the widespread application crusade types, not search promotions. So, it doesn't concern us for this course.

At last, there's the no objective choice. This is the place where you're absolutely unguided. You have your pick of any mission type, and you don't have Any custom-made proposals during the creation cycle. This ought to just be utilized by cutting edge clients who know advertisement words and promotion execution Inside and out. Also, since you're watching This video exercise the present moment, a sure thing doesn't concern Us for this exercise. We will go with leads as our mission objective.

So, I'll click that. What's more, as you can see, we would now be able to browse any of these appropriate mission types. We'll pick search advertisements and for the approaches to arrive at our objective, we'll pick site visits. We don't actually have a demo site for this exercise. So, the main Random site that flies into my head is ever lesson.com, which is a truly sweet participation slice e-learning stage. So, I'll type that in here and hit proceed. That will carry us to our mission settings page, which is the thing that we'll cover in the following exercise.

Module Two

Hi, and welcome to module two. In this module, our promotion master will tell you the best way to set up advertisement gatherings and watchword for your mission. So, prepare to take a few notes and how about we directly hop in. OK. So, we'll begin here on the mission setting screen. Since We've picked the objective, we will arrange our settings for this mission and afterward move into promotion gatherings and watchwords. In this way, first we need to give Our mission a name. I'll feel free to leave the auto-produced name they have for me here.

Next, we'll pick Which networks we need advertisements to show up on for this mission. Presently you can increase a hunt crusade with some restricted showcase network promotions, assuming you need. What's more, all things considered, Google will essentially decide pertinent arrangements around the web and stick your advertisements there with what it thinks about extra cash from your financial plan. For our motivations. We'll go on and uncheck that show alternative and spotlight on search just next is the area field. Presently this is really cool. Not exclusively would we be able to type in things like nations and urban areas, however we can even snap progress and how about we zoom in right to say Omaha, Nebraska, we'll click a sweep pin mode, and I can drop a pin and restricted my intended interest group right down to a particular number of miles from that pin. It's crazy What you can do, however for this instructional exercise, we're simply going to stay with all nations and regions Next. In case you're focusing on your crowd dependent or language, you can do that Right here. And afterward we have the spending plan. Presently the Budget is critical to comprehend this isn't a cap on everyday spending. Like a many individuals think what you're really setting here is your rough month to month spending plan separated by around 30 days. So, the genuine go through on some random day could be pretty much as much as twice what you type here and on other days it very well may be significantly not exactly that number, however Google will ensure that before one month's over, when you split everything, you will have spent this number occasions About 30. So, this will wind up being your Daily normal. Presently your genuine everyday Camp that you do have an alternative here. I need to go through as much cash as could really be expected and get these advertisements out in a more limited timeframe. Suppose you're doing retargeting for seven days long item dispatch, or you're attempting to meet a business amount or something to that effect. You can set conveyance to speed up it. So, it'll go through your cash quicker, yet know about course, that this will clearly make your spending run out ahead of schedule. Next is offering. Presently offering a promotion word is obviously, founded on the old advertisement closeout system where Google's calculations are continually choosing whose promotions to show where and when and how regularly you can pick what metric you need your offering zeroed in on here. It's naturally set to clicks, which means It'll semis for individuals really tapping on your promotions, however there's different lternatives too. Impressions allude to the number of individuals ee your promotions, whether or not they click. What's more, s you can see, there's two incredible out alternatives here for ransformations and change esteem. Presently those are quite lever to utilize, yet they expect you to set up a unique ransformation following apparatus independently first. So, we vill zero in on clicks.

We have a choice here to draw a bid line. So, in the event that ou have a particular Number as a main priority that you need to ay per click, you can enter that here. In any case, assuming you eed Google to just deal with this for you, I'll leave it clear. Next, we have start and end dates. Presently Typically advertisements ust run endlessly, yet you may have, I have a particular ustification setting an end date. For instance, in case you're running a restricted time offer or advancing a live occasion, we'll pass on this set to none for us next there's crowds.

Presently consider this. Crowds are extraordinary. You Got a great deal of segment and interest-based choices to browse here dependent on piles of information that Google has gathered, just as in view of your own information. Like in the event that you make a remarketing crowd with a following pixel, in any case, a large portion of this will be more valuable in case you're doing show advertisements for one of different sorts of promotions, and you need individuals to experience your advertisements while they're lodging Around the web. Since we're rigorously managing search advertisements in this exercise, and we in a real sense, I Want to contact individuals on the indexed lists page while they're composing explicit catchphrases, we will avoid this next.

We have expansions. Presently these are exceptionally coc site interface. Augmentations are an incredible method to ad extra connects to a hunt advertisement that connecte straightforwardly to explicit pages like you're about page or a hours of activity page get down on expansions are extraordinar for adding significant pieces of data like free transportation o item subtleties like vehicle mileage or any list item type thing that don't squeeze into the fundamental promotion text. Lastl call augmentations are in a real sense a connection that can lead straightforwardly to Call to some of your decision. We will no require any of that for our motivations yet make certain to investigate these choices. In case they're pertinent to you business. Presently it's an ideal opportunity to continue on to advertisement gatherings and Keywords. This get straightforwardly to the core of our inquiry promotion crusades What catchphrases would we like to appear for? You'll need to place a ton of thought into this since it straightforwardl influences your span. The ubiquity and recurrence of search terms is essential for clear reasons, yet you additionally need to offset that with a contest level for those pursuit terms, since that impacts the measure of your spending that gets utilized Per click. Presently there's a couple of instruments That can assist you with this, including Google's own catchphrase Planner, MAs KW locater, and SEM surge. These apparatuses can assist with getting Search volume and contest rates for referred to catchphrases, just as investigate and find extra applicable watchwords that you probably won't have considered. Whenever we've explored our watchwords, we can in a real sense simply glue them. OK here. Presently you can isolate your mission into simpler to oversee and examine bunches called advertisement gatherings. Furthermore, assuming you need to, you can have various arrangements of watchwords in each gathering. So, you can see which ones perform better get-togethers advertisement's been running for some time for this exercise, nonetheless, we'll imply require the one promotion bunch. So, I'll feel free to glue my exploration to rundown of watchwords here. There's nothing else to it for this progression. I will hit save and proceed, and we'll continue on to making the actual advertisement in the following month.

Module Three

H i, and welcome to module three. In this module, our advertisement master will tell you the best way to make your promotions and screen their exhibition after dispatch. So, prepare to take a few notes and we should directly hop in.

Good. So here We are on the advertisement creation page, you've presumably seen these item promotions around a billion times at this moment. It's your chance to make one. As we make this advertisement, watch out for this review to the here. This is the place where you can see a demo of what your advertisements will resemble on the list items page. Stage one, we need to enter the last URL that our traffic will end on. While tapping on our advertisements, staying with our superior, His model, we'll say we're sending individuals to the enrollment stage ever less than.com.

Presently we should make a few features. These are the most apparent and eye getting portions of your promotion. So, you need to ensure the main words are here, which can require a ton of thought ahead of time in light of the fact that there's a very close person limit. Suppose very simple enrollment stage and start your free preliminary and point and snap no coding.

Presently the following field here show way is discretionary. Assuming you need your customer to perceive what explicit pages or regions they're going to; you can put things here to build up the showcasing Message. Like assuming you have a dress store, you could put store.com/gosh Men's shoes slice outside or something to that effect. We don't actually have any requirement for that. So, we'll skirt this choice. Next there's depictions. Presently depictions, it could be utilized to simply pack some more additional data into your promotion since the features are really short, yet the ideal is incorporate a source of inspiration, similar to purchase now or begin Today. I think we'll attempt Get your first online course Up and running today. Presently more as of late, Google added the capacity to add one more 90 characters depiction here. That is most likely worthwhile as a rule, however I don't need mine. I promotions to get so packed with messages that the possibility's eyes miss the principal message.

So, I will stay with what we have here. That is, it. Our advertisement is done, so I'll hit done. Also, there we go. Our first inquiry promotion is all set. Presently we could Click new, add, and make a couple of more advertisements with various features, various points. And afterward we could contrast later with see which ones turn out best for this exercise. We'll stay with simply this one and I'll hit save And proceed. This carries us to the last Confirmation page, where we see a concise outline of the significant subtleties of our mission. I'll feel free to click, keep on crusading. Furthermore, here we have the dashboard for our advertisement Groups. Presently it won't be extremely useful to go over these details when everything says zero. So, we should come here to A past crusade that as of now has a few information for us to discuss. So here we have an advertisement bunch from past crusade that as of now has a few positions related with it. This one was a test crusade for selling Instruments. Here. You can monitor a huge load of significant stuff. For instance, we have the, the real catchphrases themselves alongside a switch button for empowering or stopping every individual watchword. We have your maximum CPC. In the event that you set it, regardless of whether your catchphrase was endorsed, But the main information is somewhere in this vicinity. We have your number of snaps impressions, which implies the number of individuals saw your promotions for those catchphrases Click through rate normal expense per click and the all-out cost from that watchword up until now. So, to take one of these for instance, the term Violin deal has gotten five ticks to our site. So far that is out of 148 individuals who have seen the advertisement, which gives us a tick pace of three dabs, 8%. Presently, in light of the manner in which Google was dealing with our offering, we wound up Spending $3 and 29 pennies for those five ticks, which gives us a normal expense for each snap of 66 pennies. From that catchphrase, as should be obvious, this mission was in its outset, however you ought to screen these details routinely on the grounds that after some time with more information, the normal has gotten more certain. What's more, the distinctions in execution between catchphrases become all the clearer. On the off chance that you confirm that specific catchphrases aren't playing out that well, or that there's sufficiently not search volume, and you need to center your spending plan somewhere else, you can stop singular watchwords here with this Toggle alternative. Also, the writing is on the wall. We've succeeded. He made an inquiry promoting effort.

Don't miss out!

Visit the website below and you can sign up to receive emails whenever B. Vincent publishes a new book. There's no charge and no obligation.

https://books2read.com/r/B-A-QWUO-XBDRB

Also by B. Vincent

Bookkeeping
Bridge Pages
Business Acquisition
Business Bogging
Marketing Automation
Better Meetings
Business Conflict Resolution
Conversion Optimization
Creative Solutions
Employee Recruitment
Startup Capital
Employee Mentoring
Followership
Servant Leadership
Human Resources
Team Building
Freelancing
Funnel Building
Geo Targeting
Goal Setting
Immanent List Building
Lead Generation
Leadership Course
Leadership Transition
LinkedIn Ads
LinkedIn Marketing
Messenger Marketing
New Management
Newsfeed Ads
Search Ads
Online Learning

Sales Webinars
Side Hustles
Split Testing
Twitter Timeline Advertising

About the Publisher

Accepting manuscripts in the most categories. We love to help people get their words available to the world.

Revival Waves of Glory focus is to provide more options to be published. We do traditional paperbacks, hardcovers, audio books and ebooks all over the world. A traditional royalty-based publisher that offers self-publishing options, Revival Waves provides a very author friendly and transparent publishing process, with President Bill Vincent involved in the full process of your book. Send us your manuscript and we will contact you as soon as possible.

Contact: Bill Vincent at rwgpublishing@yahoo.com www.rwgpublishing.com